Presented to

_____

Given by

_____

TWELVE SACRED SONGS
IN WORD AND MUSIC

HYMNS OF
devotion

DANIEL PARTNER

BARBOUR
PUBLISHING, INC.

Published by Barbour Publishing, Inc., P.O. Box 719, Uhrichsville, Ohio 44683
www.barbourbooks.com

ecpa Member of the
Evangelical Christian
Publishers Association

Printed in China.

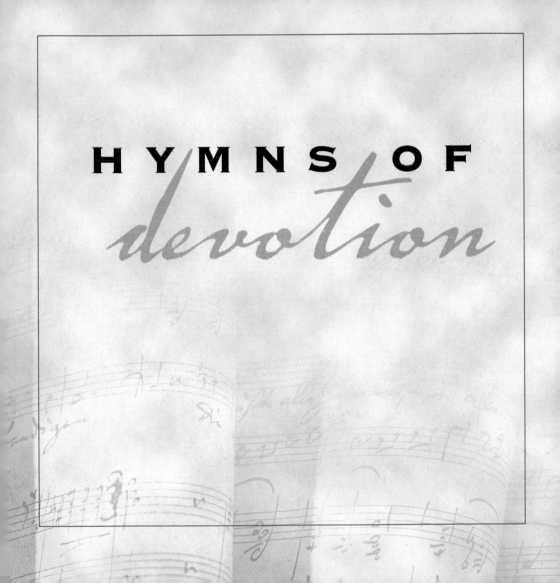

As the deer pants
for streams of water,
so I long for you,
O God.

THESE words of an ancient poet are found in the Bible as the first verse of Psalm 42—one of 150 poems in the Book of Psalms. The Psalms were the hymns of the ancient Jews. They provide a precious glimpse into the hearts of those who were seeking God in olden days.

Modern times are entirely different than those the psalmist knew. Yet people haven't changed that much—the human heart still longs for God. This longing is heard in the hymns we sing in worship—like these lines written by Annie Hawks:

I need Thee, O I need Thee;
Every hour I need Thee.

Hawks's expression of devotion to God describes the essence of Christian spirituality.

This little book is full of such beautiful devotional thoughts and feelings. Here are the lyrics to twelve great hymns of devotion to God. The lyrics are combined with a brief writing detailing the meaning of the hymn and the experiences of its author. You will find the music to these hymns on the compact disk enclosed in this package. I pray that this poetry and music will enhance your enjoyment of the Spirit and deepen your love for God.

Daniel Partner
Sisters, Oregon

Take My Life and Let It Be

Words: Frances Ridley Havergal

Music: Anonymous

Take my life and let it be

Con - se - cra - ted, Lord, to Thee;

Take my mo - ments and my days,

Let them flow in cease - less praise.

TAKE MY LIFE
AND LET IT BE

Take my life, and let it be consecrated, Lord, to Thee.
Take my moments and my days; let them flow in
ceaseless praise.
Take my hands, and let them move at the impulse of Thy love.
Take my feet, and let them be swift and beautiful for Thee.

Take my voice, and let me sing always, only, for my King.
Take my lips, and let them be filled with messages from Thee.
Take my silver and my gold; not a mite would I withhold.
Take my intellect, and use every power as Thou shalt choose.

Take my will, and make it Thine; it shall be no longer mine.
Take my heart, it is Thine own; it shall be Thy royal throne.
Take my love, my Lord, I pour at Thy feet its treasure store.
Take myself, and I will be ever, only, all for Thee.

And so,
dear brothers and sisters,
I plead with you to give your bodies to God.

*Let them be a living and holy
sacrifice—the kind he will accept.
When you think of what he has done for you,
is this too much to ask?*

Romans 12:1

"**I WENT** (to Areley House) for a little visit of five days," recalled Frances Havergal. "There were ten persons in the house, some unconverted and long prayed for, some converted, but not rejoicing Christians. [The Lord] gave me the prayer, 'Lord, give me all in this house!' And he just did. Before I left the house every one had got a blessing. The last night of my visit after I had retired, the governess asked me to go to the two daughters. They were crying. Then and there both of them trusted and rejoiced; it was nearly midnight. I was too happy to sleep, and passed most of the night in praise and renewal of my own consecration; and these little couplets formed themselves, and chimed in my heart one after another till they finished with 'Ever, only, all for Thee!' "

Those are the final words of Havergal's cherished hymn. With the first lines she sings, "Take my life and let it be consecrated, Lord to Thee." The word *consecrated* means devoted entirely, dedicated. Havergal goes on to list everything she desires the Lord to take—moments and days, hands and feet, voice and lips, silver and gold, intellect and will, heart and love—a very complete list. Its sum: her entire self.

The key word in this hymn is *take*. Havergal is submitting herself to God. She is simply making herself available to God. She is simply making herself available for the divine purpose. She is not insisting; she is not presumptuous. No one can demand to be used by God. The best we can do is be available to God, praying, "Take me."

Frances R. Havergal was born in Worcestershire, England, and educated there and in Düsseldorf, Germany. She wrote many hymns that emphasize faith, devotion, and service to God. She was the master of several languages, including Latin, Hebrew, Greek, French, and German. She was a natural musician with a pleasing, well-trained voice and a brilliant hand at the piano. This extraordinary woman was also a devoted Bible student who memorized large sections of Scripture. She practiced a disciplined prayer life and noted in her Bible the times and topics of her prayers. She described her way of writing hymns this way: "Writing is praying with me, for I never seem to write even a verse by myself, and feel like a little child writing; you know a child would look up at every sentence and say, 'And what shall I say next?' That is just what I do; I ask that at every line he would give me not merely thoughts and power, but also every word, even the very rhymes. Very often I have a most distinct and happy consciousness of direct answers."

She is called the "consecration poet" because her hymns often emphasize one's complete dedication to God. Significantly, her namesake is Nicholas Ridley, a prominent Bishop martyred at Oxford in 1555. Although she died 120 years ago, Havergal's hymns are still loved and sung today. Other hymns by Frances Havergal include

"Who Is on the Lord's Side?", "Thou Art Coming, O My Savior," and "I Am Trusting Thee, Lord Jesus." A volume of her verse, entitled *Poetical Works,* was published in 1884. Her prose writings include *Kept for the Master's Use* and *Royal Commandments and Royal Bounty.*

Lord, take my will; make it yours, and it will not be
mine anymore. Take my heart; it is yours.
Make it into your throne.
Take my love, Lord; it is my only treasure.
I pour it at your feet. And I pray that one day
you will take my entire self.
Then I will be ever, only, and all for you.

One of the Pharisees asked Jesus
to come to his home for a meal,

so Jesus accepted the invitation and sat down to eat.
A certain immoral woman heard he was there and brought
a beautiful jar filled with expensive perfume.
Then she knelt behind him at his feet, weeping.
Her tears fell on his feet,
and she wiped them off with her hair.
Then she kept kissing his feet and putting perfume on them.

Luke 7:36–38

Fill Thou My Life

Words: Horatius Bonar

Music: Thomas Haweis

Fill Thou my life, O Lord my God, In ev - 'ry part with praise, That my whole be - ing may pro - claim Thy be - ing and Thy ways.

FILL THOU MY LIFE

Fill Thou my life, O Lord my God,
In every part with praise,
That my whole being may proclaim
Thy being and Thy ways.
Not for the lip of praise alone,
Nor e'en the praising heart
I ask, but for a life made up
Of praise in every part!

Praise in the common words I speak,
Life's common looks and tones,
In fellowship in hearth and board
With my beloved ones;
Not in the temple crowd alone
Where holy voices chime,
But in the silent paths of earth,
The quiet rooms of time.

That is why
    I can never stop
        praising you;

I declare your glory all day long.
      Psalm 71:8

HORATIUS Bonar is called "the prince of Scottish hymn writers" and wrote the lyrics to over six hundred hymns. He descended from a long line of Scottish preachers, graduated from the University of Edinburgh, was ordained and became pastor of the North Parish, Kelso, in 1838. He joined the Free Church of Scotland during the "Disruption" of 1843, when evangelicals departed the staunchly Presbyterian Church of Scotland. Bonar remained in Kelso for twenty-eight years. He moved to the Chalmers Memorial church in Edinburgh and served there until his death.

During a memorial service for Horatius Bonar, his friend,

Rev. E. H. Lundie, said: "His hymns were written in very varied circumstances, sometimes timed by the tinkling brook that babbled near him; sometimes attuned to the ordered tramp of the ocean, whose crested waves broke on the beach by which he wandered; sometimes set to the rude music of the railway train that hurried him to the scene of duty; sometimes measured by the silent rhythm of the midnight stars that shone above him."

Bonar's hymn "Fill Thou My Life" is his extended prayer for complete devotion to God. He prayed "not for the lip of praise alone, nor e'en the praising heart I ask, but for a life made up of praise in every part!" That was quite an order, although it is in full accord with the hope of the gospel.

For example, the apostle Paul prayed for the believers in Philippi like this: "I thank my God in all my remembrance of you, always in every prayer of mine for you all making my prayer with joy, thankful for your partnership in the gospel from the first day until now" (Philippians 1:3–5 RSV). Paul's prayer encompassed a period of time that began the first day he met the Philippians. Paul did not expect immediate change to come upon these people. For anyone to have a "life made up of praise in every part" is a lifelong project.

Paul continues: "It is right for me to feel thus about you all, because I hold you in my heart, for you are all partakers with me of grace, both in my imprisonment and in the defense and confirmation of the gospel" (v. 7). Here is the important phrase—*partakers with me of grace*. The problem is that none of us will have the opportunity to support Paul in his imprisonment. We can't partake of that grace. A few may get to find grace in the defense and confirmation of the gospel, but not many. So what are the rest of us to do?

Listen as Paul prays on. "For God is my witness, how I yearn for you all with the affection of Christ Jesus. And it is my prayer that your love may abound more and more, with knowledge and all discernment, so that you may approve what is excellent, and may be pure and blameless for the day of Christ, filled with the fruits of righteousness which come through Jesus Christ, to the glory and praise of God" (vv. 8–11).

In his prayer, Paul is looking forward to the day of Christ, the day Jesus returns. He asks God that on that day we would bear the ripened fruit of righteousness. And the goal? It is the same as that of Horatius Bonar—to the glory and praise of God.

Until that day, how do we partake of grace? There are many

ways. You might try this: Each time you shop for groceries, buy some non-perishable items to give to the poor. Perhaps ten percent of your total purchase could go to others. You may want to pray for those less fortunate as you buy these things. In this way you will partake of grace and in you, the fruit of righteousness will ripen.

. . .

Lord, forgive me for seeking to have more
for myself while I forget the needy.
Soften my heart toward the poor,
and open it to share with the hungry.

In fact,
James, Peter, and John,
who were known as pillars of the church,

recognized the gift God had given me,
and they accepted Barnabas and me
as their co-workers.
They encouraged us to keep preaching
to the Gentiles, while they continued their work
with the Jews.

The only thing they suggested
was that we remember

to help the poor,

and I have certainly been eager
to do that.

Galatians 2:9–10

Jesus, I Come

Words: William T. Sleeper

Music: George C. Stebbins

Out of my bond - age, sor - row and night, Je - sus, I come,

Je - sus, I come; In - to Thy free - dom, glad - ness and light,

Je - sus, I come to Thee. Out of my sick - ness

in - to Thy health, Out of my want and in - to Thy wealth,

Out of my sin and in - to Thy-self, Je - sus, I come to Thee.

JESUS, I COME

Out of my bondage, sorrow, and night,
 Jesus, I come, Jesus, I come;
Into Thy freedom, gladness, and light,
 Jesus, I come to Thee;
Out of my sickness, into Thy health,
Out of my want and into Thy wealth,
Out of my sin and into Thyself,
 Jesus, I come to Thee.

Out of my shameful failure and loss,
 Jesus, I come, Jesus, I come;
Into the glorious gain of Thy cross,
 Jesus, I come to Thee.
Out of earth's sorrows into Thy balm,
Out of life's storms and into Thy calm,
Out of distress to jubilant psalm,
 Jesus, I come to Thee.

From the depths of despair,
O Lord, I call for your help.
Psalm 130:1

THERE is something to be said for self-esteem, but it is not of much use in knowing God.

Originally people were friendly with God. The garden in Eden was given to them to care for; it was theirs to enjoy (see Genesis 2:15). Adam possessed the genius to name all the animals and the sensitivity to know that he was lonely (vv. 18–24). The original couple even knew just where to go in the evening to find God walking in the cool of the garden (Gen. 3:8). And "although Adam and his wife were both naked, neither of them felt any shame" (Gen. 2:25). In other words, they were not self-aware, they had no self-esteem.

They did esteem God. But soon they were tempted away from their adoration to partake the fruit of a forbidden tree (Gen. 3:6). They were deceived into believing that they did not need God. Infected with arrogance, they lost their innocence. From there, human culture developed independent of the Creator. In fact, our culture is a replacement for all that God is.

Then the day came when God entered this world of pride like a tender green shoot sprouting in dry and sterile ground. God was born in a little hill-town and given the name Jesus. He seemed to be just another child. There was nothing beautiful or majestic about his appearance, nothing to attract people to him (see Isaiah 53:2).

In time the God-man could no longer be overlooked. Yet Jesus was despised and rejected. He was a man of sorrows, familiar with bitterest grief. We turned our backs on him. We looked the other way when he went by. He was despised and we didn't care (v. 3).

Then came a day when all this seemed to turn around. Jesus attended a festival in Jerusalem and people thronged to him with praises. That was on a bright Sunday morning. By Friday of the same week he was betrayed, arrested, and abandoned to face the cruel end.

First Jesus was beaten nearly to death. Then, along with two criminals, he was crucified. People came out to see the spectacle. Some of them shouted abusively at Jesus, wagging their heads in mockery. "If you are the Son of God," they laughed, "save yourself and come down from the cross!" He silently hung by his arms, slowly suffocating.

Leading priests, religious teachers, and other important men made sport of the dying man. "He saved others," they scoffed, "but he can't save himself! This is the king of Israel? Come down from the cross, and we will believe in you! You trusted God—Why doesn't God deliver you? You're the one who said, 'I am the Son of God.'" The criminals who were crucified somehow found the strength to shout the same insults (see Matthew 27:38–44).

That was when the arrogance our ancestors showed in the garden bore its fruit in fullness. Blinded by pride, who could know that it was our weaknesses he carried; it was our sorrows that weighed him down. We thought his troubles were a punishment from God for his own sins. Not so. He was wounded and crushed for our sins. He was beaten that we could have peace. When he was whipped, we were healed (see Isaiah 53:4–5).

William True Sleeper's hymn "Out Of My Bondage, Sorrow, and Night" expresses that healing. These are the words of someone cured from the arrogant attitude that believed "God is superfluous."

Out of my shameful failure and loss,
Jesus, I come, Jesus, I come;
Into the glorious gain of Thy cross,
Jesus, I come to Thee.

Jesus, I come to you out of the depths
of untold ruin and into your sheltering peace.
Jesus, I come to you.

He brought them out and asked,

"Sirs, what must I do to be saved?"

They replied, "Believe on the Lord Jesus
and you will be saved,
along with your entire household."
Then they shared the word of the
Lord with him and all who lived in his household.
That same hour the jailer washed their wounds,
and he and everyone in his household
were immediately baptized.

Acts 16:30–33

Just As I Am

Words: Charlotte Elliott

Music: William B. Bradbury

Just as I am, with-out one plea But that Thy blood was shed for me, And that Thou bidd'st me come to Thee, O Lamb of God, I come! I come!

Just As I Am

Just as I am, without one plea,
But that Thy blood was shed for me,
And that Thou bidst me come to Thee,
O Lamb of God, I come, I come.

Just as I am, and waiting not
To rid my soul of one dark blot,
To Thee whose blood can cleanse each spot,
O Lamb of God, I come, I come.

Just as I am, though tossed about
With many a conflict, many a doubt,
Fightings and fears within, without,
O Lamb of God, I come, I come.

Just as I am, poor, wretched, blind;
Sight, riches, healing of the mind,
Yea, all I need in Thee to find,
O Lamb of God, I come, I come.

Have mercy on me, O God,
because of your unfailing love.

Because of your great compassion,
blot out the stain of my sins.

Wash me clean from my guilt.
Purify me from my sin.

Psalm 51:1–2

CHARLOTTE Elliott's brother was a Christian minister. Here is what he said about the hymn "Just As I Am": "In the course of a long ministry, I hope I have been permitted to see some of the fruit of my labor, but I feel that far more has been done by a single hymn of my sister's."

Elliott's hymn contains the same message as does a story told about two men who went up to the temple to pray. One was a Pharisee and the other a tax collector. "The proud Pharisee stood by himself and prayed this prayer: 'I thank you, God, that I am not a sinner like everyone else, especially like that tax collector over there! For I never cheat, I don't sin, I don't commit adultery, I fast twice a week, and I give you a tenth of my income.'

"But the tax collector stood at a distance and dared not even lift his eyes to heaven as he prayed. Instead, he beat his chest in sorrow, saying, 'O God, be merciful to me, for I am a sinner' " (Luke 18:11–13).

Jesus tells the lesson of his story—"I tell you, this sinner, not the Pharisee, returned home justified before God. For the proud will be humbled, but the humble will be honored" (Luke 18:14).

One of these men was humble, the other was self-exalting. What was the Pharisee so exultant about? His own goodness. Why was the tax collector so humble? He knew he was a sinner. In fact, they were both sinners, but only one admitted it.

If you think you must be on your best behavior to come to God, remember this: Your best is not good enough. Jesus said, "No one is good but God alone" (Mark 10:18 RSV). God is not like Santa Claus who, as the old poem says, keeps a list of naughty and nice. God has no need of such a list since "all have sinned; all fall short of God's glorious standard" (Romans 3:23).

No amount of self-improvement can bring you to the level of God. For this reason everyone must sing, "Just as I am, without one plea, but that your blood was shed for me, and that you bid me come to Thee, O Lamb of God, I come, I come!"

The hymn was written after Charlotte Elliott heard the truth of the gospel from the Swiss evangelist Cèsar Malan. She not only believed in Jesus, she wrote this most popular of gospel hymns. For twenty-five years Elliott was editor of the annual *Christian Remembrancer Pocketbook* and she assisted in the publication of the *Invalid's Hymn Book,* which contained 112 of her poems. She wrote 150 hymns that address the concerns of those in sickness and sorrow.

Dear Lord, save me from being haughty like the praying Pharisee and let me know your love as you receive me just as I am.

*But now you belong
to Christ Jesus.
Though you once were
far away from God,*

*now you have been
brought near to him*

because of the blood of Christ.
Ephesians 2:13

I Am Thine, O Lord

Words: Fanny J. Crosby

Music: W. H. Doane

I am Thine, O Lord, I have heard Thy voice, And it told Thy love to me; But I long to rise in the arms of faith, And be clos - er drawn to Thee.

Refrain

Draw me near - er, near - er, bless - ed Lord, To the cross where Thou hast died; Draw me near - er, near - er, near - er, bless - ed Lord, To Thy pre - cious, bleed - ing side.

I Am Thine, O Lord

I am Thine, O Lord, I have heard Thy voice,
And it told Thy love to me;
But I long to rise in the arms of faith
And be closer drawn to Thee.

Consecrate me now to Thy service, Lord,
By the power of grace divine;
Let my soul look up with a steadfast hope,
And my will be lost in Thine.

Refrain
Draw me nearer, nearer blessed Lord,
To the cross where Thou hast died.
Draw me nearer, nearer, nearer blessed Lord,
To Thy precious, bleeding side.

"The eye is the lamp of the body.

So, if your eye is healthy, *your whole body* *will be full of light."*

Matthew 6:22 NRSV

"I AM Thine, O Lord" is one of the best-loved of the hymns written by Fanny Crosby. Born Frances Jane Crosby in Putnam County, New York, Fanny lost her eyesight at six weeks of age while being treated by an incompetent doctor. She was blind for the remainder of her life. Here is one of her earliest poems:

Oh, what a happy soul I am,
Although I cannot see!
I am resolved that in this world
Contented I will be.
How many blessings I enjoy
That other people don't;
To weep and sigh because I'm blind,
I cannot and I won't!

Crosby was educated at the New York Institute for the Blind and was a student of composer George F. Root; she wrote lyrics for some of his popular songs. The number of hymns and poems Crosby wrote has been variously reported—anywhere between four and eight thousand. Her hymns are found in nearly every modern American hymnal.

Her hymns are proof that, though blind, Fanny Crosby had a spiritual vision like few others. She said, "It seemed intended by the blessed providence of God that I should be blind all my life, and I thank him for the dispensation. If perfect earthly sight were offered me tomorrow, I would not accept it. I might not have sung hymns to the praise of God if I had been distracted by the beautiful and interesting things about me."

Once she said to a minister, "Do you know that if at birth I had been able to make one petition, it would have been that I should be born blind?"

"Why?" asked the surprised pastor.

"Because when I get to heaven," she responded, "the first face that shall ever gladden my sight will be that of my Savior!"

Later she wrote, "When I remember his mercy and loving kindness; when I have been blessed above the common lot of mortals; and when happiness has touched the deep places of my soul—how can I repine? And I have often thought of the passage of Scripture: 'The light of the body is the eye, if therefore, thine eye be single thy whole body shall be full of light.' "

If blindness freed Crosby from distractions, she eagerly learned to turn that freedom into meditation. She wrote, "Most of my poems have been written during the long night watches when the distractions of the day could not interfere with the rapid flow of thought. . . .

"That some of my hymns have been dictated by the blessed Holy Spirit, I have no doubt. That others have been the result of deep meditation, I know to be true. But that the poet has any right to claim special merit for himself is certainly presumptuous. I have sometimes felt that there is a deep and clear well of inspiration from which one may draw the sparkling draughts that are so essential to good poetry. At times the burden of inspiration is so heavy that the author himself cannot find words beautiful enough or thoughts deep enough for its expression. . . .

"The most enduring hymns are born in the silences of the soul and nothing must be allowed to intrude while they are being framed into language. Some of the sweetest melodies of the heart never see the light of the printed page. Sometimes the song without words has a deeper meaning than the most elaborate combinations of words and music."

. . .

Dear God, thank you for all the
gifted people you have given to your church.
I pray you will give grace to everyone
who seeks you, so that they too may
become gifts in this poor world.

"*I know this:*
I was blind,

and now I can see!"
John 9:25

May the Mind of Christ, My Savior

Words: Kate B. Wilkinson

Music: A. Cyril Barham-Gould

May the mind of Christ my Sav - ior
Live in me from day to day, By His love and
pow'r con - trol - ling All I do and say.

MAY THE MIND OF CHRIST, MY SAVIOR

May the mind of Christ, my Savior, live in me from day to day,
By His love and power controlling all I do and say.

May the Word of God dwell richly in my heart from hour to hour,
So that all may see I triumph only through His power.

May the peace of God my Father rule my life in everything,
That I may be calm to comfort sick and sorrowing.

May the love of Jesus fill me as the waters fill the sea;
Him exalting, self abasing, this is victory.

May I run the race before me, strong and brave to face the foe,
Looking only unto Jesus as I onward go.

May His beauty rest upon me, as I seek the lost to win,
And may they forget the channel, seeing only Him.

Pray in the Spirit
at all times
in every prayer and supplication.
Ephesians 6:18 NRSV

THERE was a time when serious difficulties came to my family. I prayed, and things got worse. After fifteen years of praying, I gave it up. I didn't think I knew how anymore. At such times the Holy Spirit helps us in our distress. "For we don't even know what we should pray for, nor how we should pray. But the Holy Spirit prays for us with groanings that cannot be expressed in words" (Romans 8:26). Believe it or not, this is what happens in times of prayerless distress.

However, at the times you *can* pray, here is a secret to having your prayers answered: simply ask for the things that God wants to give to you. For example, my daughter has a five-year-old son named Uriah. While I was talking with my daughter on the telephone one day, I heard Uriah ask his mother if he could have some tofu to eat. (You may know that tofu is a cheese made from processed soybeans.)

She gladly gave him the tofu. If Uriah had asked his mother for candy, she'd have surely turned him down.

How do you know what God wants to give you? Use the Scripture as a guide to your petitions. The hymn "May the Mind of Christ, My Savior" is really several separate prayers. Each prayer is drawn from the Scripture; each is a good example of a prayer that is according to God's heart.

First Kate Wilkinson, author of the hymn, prays, "May the mind of Christ, my Savior, live in me from day to day." This request is drawn from Philippians 2:5—"Let the same mind be in you that was in Christ Jesus" (NRSV). If you wish to pray this prayer, continue to pray using the following verses: Philippians 2:6–8—"Though he was God, he did not demand and cling to his rights as God. He made himself nothing; he took the humble position of a slave and appeared in human form. And in human form he obediently humbled himself even further by dying a criminal's death on a cross." This describes the mind of Christ.

The hymn's second verse asks, "May the word of God dwell richly in my heart from hour to hour." This is a rephrasing of Colossians

3:16 (NRSV)–"Let the word of Christ dwell in you richly." Verse three of the hymn asks, "May the peace of God my Father rule my life in everything." Here is the verse this prayer comes from: "Do not worry about anything, but in everything by prayer and supplication with thanksgiving let your requests be made known to God, and the peace of God, which surpasses all understanding, will guard your hearts and your minds in Christ Jesus" (Philippians 4:6–7 NRSV).

The prayer of verse four is "May the love of Jesus fill me as the waters fill the sea." Wilkinson drew this from Ephesians 3:19–"Know the love of Christ that surpasses knowledge, so that you may be filled with all the fullness of God" (NRSV). Verse five of the hymn rephrases Hebrews 12:1–"Therefore, since we are surrounded by such a huge crowd of witnesses to the life of faith, let us strip off every weight that slows us down, especially the sin that so easily hinders our progress. And let us run with endurance the race that God has set before us."

Finally the hymn asks for Christ's beauty. Here is a verse you may use to pray with such a sentiment–"Our lives are a fragrance presented by Christ to God. But this fragrance is perceived differently by those being saved and by those perishing. To those who are per-ishing we are a fearful smell of death and doom. But to those who are being saved we are a life-giving perfume" (2 Corinthians 2:15–16).

Thank you, dear God,
for the riches found in the Bible.
Teach me to use the words of Scripture
for my prayers; and hear these prayers,
I ask, for the glory of your name.

How we praise God,
the Father
of our Lord Jesus Christ,

who has blessed us with every spiritual blessing
in the heavenly realms because we belong to Christ.

Long ago,
even before he made the world,

God loved us and chose us in Christ to be holy
and without fault in his eyes.
Ephesians 1:3–4

Who Is on the Lord's Side?

Words: Frances R. Havergal

Music: Sir John Goss

Who is on the Lord's side? Who will serve the King? Who will be His help - ers, Oth - er lives to bring? Who will leave the world's side? Who will face the foe? Who is on the Lord's side? Who for Him will go? By Thy call of mer - cy, By Thy grace di - vine, We are on the Lord's side, Sav - iour, we are Thine.

WHO IS ON THE LORD'S SIDE?

Who is on the Lord's side? Who will serve the King?
Who will be His helpers, other lives to bring?
Who will leave the world's side? Who will face the foe?
Who is on the Lord's side? Who for Him will go?
By Thy call of mercy, by Thy grace divine,
We are on the Lord's side—Savior, we are Thine!

Not for weight of glory, nor for crown and palm,
Enter we the army, raise the warrior psalm;
But for love that claimeth lives for whom He died:
He whom Jesus nameth must be on His side.
By Thy love constraining, by Thy grace divine,
We are on the Lord's side—Savior, we are Thine!

He stood at the entrance
to the camp and shouted,

"All of you who are
on the LORD'S side,
come over here and join me."

And all the Levites came.
Exodus 32:26

FRANCES Ridley Havergal was a frail woman, sick and unable to work for much of her adult life. But she certainly did write an aggressive, militant hymn in "Who is On the Lord's Side?" Its theme of warfare appears often in the favorite hymns of the church. "Onward Christian Soldiers," written for a children's Sunday school event, may be the best-known. Martin Luther's "A Mighty Fortress Is Our God" is the classic of this genre. And no one more than Luther has ever so fiercely battled the enemy of God. Although these hymns are wonderful in their own way, the book of Ephesians is the believer's ultimate reference on the subject of spiritual warfare.

Luther, in the first verse of his hymn, warned that on earth there is no equal to our ancient foe. But Ephesians says, "Be strong in the Lord and in the strength of his might" (6:10 RSV). Christ is the believer's armor. Therefore "put on the whole armor of God, that you may be able to stand against the wiles of the devil" (v. 11 RSV).

But before you start, there is a vital fact you must remember: "We are not contending against flesh and blood, but against the principalities, against the powers, against the world rulers of this present darkness, against the spiritual hosts of wickedness in the heavenly places" (v. 12 RSV). In other words, the Lord's enemies are not people. Do not fight with doctors, politicians, teachers, Hollywood filmmakers, or anyone else who seems to oppose the Lord. Remember, this is spiritual warfare. It is not physical or psychological.

So "be strong in the Lord and in the strength of his might." In other words, put on the marvelous armor of God. Around your middle is the strengthening belt of truth. Your heart is covered with the breastplate of righteousness. For shoes you wear the gospel of peace. On your left arm is the shield of faith "with which you can quench all the flaming darts of the evil one." Your thoughts are protected by the helmet of salvation. Your right hand holds the sword of the Spirit, which is the word of God (see vv. 14–17 RSV).

Truth, righteousness, the gospel of peace, faith, salvation, and the word of God—these together protect your entire being.

But how to put on this armor? Do you think this detail would be neglected? Here's the way: "Pray at all times in the Spirit, with all prayer and supplication" (v. 18 RSV). Pray to understand the truth. Pray and receive the gift of God's righteousness. Petition for the advancement of the gospel, for the increase of your faith, and for the understanding of your salvation.

"Where would I get the utterance for all these prayers?" you may ask. Use the words of the Bible instead of your own. After all, the sword of the Spirit is the word of God.

. . .

Lord, by your grace

you've made me willing

and by your redemption

you've made me free. I'm on your side.

Savior, I'm yours!

*God disarmed
the evil rulers*
and authorities.

He shamed them publicly
by his victory
over them on the cross of Christ.
Colossians 2:15

I Am Trusting Thee, Lord Jesus

Words: Frances R. Havergal

Music: Ethelbert W. Bullinger

I am trust - ing Thee, Lord Je - sus—
Trust - ing on - ly, Thee; Trust - ing Thee for
full sal - va - tion, Great and free.

I AM TRUSTING THEE,
LORD JESUS

I am trusting Thee, Lord, Jesus, trusting only Thee;
Trusting Thee for full salvation, great and free.

I am trusting Thee for pardon; at Thy feet I bow;
For Thy grace and tender mercy, trusting now.

I am trusting Thee for cleansing in the crimson flood;
Trusting Thee to make me holy by Thy blood.

I am trusting Thee to guide me; Thou alone shalt lead;
Every day and hour supplying all my need.

I am trusting Thee for power, Thine can never fail;
Words which Thou Thyself shalt give me must prevail.

I am trusting Thee, Lord Jesus; never let me fall;
I am trusting Thee forever, and for all.

And that is why I am suffering
here in prison.
But I am not ashamed of it,
for I know the one in whom I trust,

and I am sure that he is able to guard
what I have entrusted to him

until the day
of his return.

2 Timothy 1:12

WHEN I came to believe in Christ I had many reasons to do so. The one that I think tipped the scale was the happiness of a friend. I didn't know Bill well, but we had mutual friends and I saw him from time to time. One day I happened upon him in our little town. He was happier than I could imagine anyone being. His face shone with it. His voice was one of joy. This was so striking because the last time I had seen Bill I could tell from a distance that he was deeply miserable. His appearance made me fear to go near him and risk contamination by his misery. I didn't see Bill for the entire summer. Then in October he reappeared, transformed. He came to me and said three words: "Christ is real." In three days, I, too, trusted.

As I said, there were many reasons why I believed in Christ. But my friend Bill embodied irrefutable evidence. At the time he was my guarantee that Christ is real.

Twenty-seven years later I was driving with my son out of the Bitterroot Mountains into southeastern Idaho when we stopped at a fruit stand amidst an orchard. Peaches were in season and there they were, arrayed for sale in boxes and bags. I asked the owner of the stand if the peaches were ready to eat. He brought out his pocketknife, picked up a peach, and without a word sliced it and gave it to me to eat. It was deliciously sweet and juicy as only a peach can be. I couldn't help myself. I bought a bushel box and shoehorned it into my overloaded car. The man had used not one word to convince me. Instead he gave me a taste to guarantee that his were astounding peaches.

That is why we trust the Bible's good news. We've been given a guarantee we will receive all it promises. For example, it says, "Our dying bodies make us groan and sigh, but it's not that we want to die and have no bodies at all. We want to slip into our new bodies so that these dying bodies will be swallowed up by everlasting life" (2 Corinthians 5:4).

Slip into our new bodies? Sounds crazy. Be swallowed up by everlasting life? That's farfetched; how can anyone believe it? Here's why we can: "God himself has prepared us for this, and as a guarantee he has given us his Holy Spirit" (v. 5). Just as I tasted a little slice of a peach, so I tasted the Spirit when I believed. I know whom I have trusted and his flavor is always in me and will be until I receive the promised inheritance in full.

Lord, I know that no eye has seen,
no ear has heard, and no mind has imagined
what God has prepared for those who love him.
So I only ask that you will give me a
foretaste of these things so I can persevere
through this world of suffering.

The Spirit is
God's guarantee
that he will give us everything
he promised

and that he has purchased us
to be his own people.

This is just one more reason
for us to praise
our glorious God.

Ephesians 1:14

O Master, Let Me Walk with Thee

Words: Washington Gladden

Music: H. Percy Smith

O Mas - ter, let me walk with Thee

In low - ly paths of ser - vice free;

Tell me Thy se - cret; help me bear The

strain of toil, the fret of care.

O MASTER,
LET ME WALK WITH THEE

O Master, let me walk with Thee,
In lowly paths of service free;
Tell me Thy secret; help me bear
The strain of toil, the fret of care.

Help me the slow of heart to move
By some clear, winning word of love;
Teach me the wayward feet to stay,
And guide them in the homeward way.

O Master, let me walk with Thee,
Before the taunting Pharisee;
Help me to bear the sting of spite,
The hate of men who hide Thy light.

No, O people,
the LORD has already told you
what is good,
and this is what he requires:
to do what is right,
to love mercy,
and to walk humbly with your God.
Micah 6:8

REMEMBER this refrain?

> *Just a closer walk with thee.*
> *Grant it, Jesus, is my plea,*
> *Daily walking close to thee,*
> *Let it be, dear Lord, let it be.*

It is hard to tell what is meant when someone speaks of "walking with God," since the Bible says very little about this. But the Gospel of Luke does tell a story of a walk with God. It occurred on the day of Christ's resurrection. Two of Jesus' followers were walking to Emmaus, a village about seven miles from Jerusalem. As they walked along they were talking about everything that had happened over the past week or so. Suddenly, Jesus came along and joined the two, walking beside them. But they didn't know who he was. Luke says this was because "their eyes were kept from recognizing him" (Luke 24:16 RSV).

"You seem to be in a deep discussion about something," he said. "What are you so concerned about?" They stopped short, sadness written across their faces. Then one of them, Cleopas, replied, "You must be the only person in Jerusalem who hasn't heard about all the things that have happened there the last few days."

"What things?" Jesus asked.

"The things that happened to Jesus, the man from Nazareth," they said (vv. 17–19). The two then recited everything they knew about Jesus. Yet they didn't recognize him walking beside them.

When the three approached Emmaus, Jesus would have walked on, but the two disciples begged him to stay there with them. So he went to their home and sat down to a meal. Jesus took a small loaf of bread, asked God's blessing on it, broke it, and gave it to them to eat.

Suddenly, they recognized him. And at that moment he disappeared! (see vv. 20–31).

This describes a common problem of walking with the Lord–you are unaware that the Lord is actually with you. Why is this? These two men knew a lot about Jesus (see vv. 19–24). Yet, the Lord scolded them for being foolish and "slow of heart to believe all the prophets have declared" (v. 25 NRSV). Knowing about Christ is not of much use for a daily walk with Christ. But believing the Scriptures is indispensable.

For example, Jesus said, "I am the bread of life. . .so whoever eats me will live because of me" (John 6:35, 57 NRSV). The men eating with Jesus in Emmaus recognized him when he fed them. When you eat the "words of eternal life" (v. 68 NRSV), your life is changed. The apostle Paul's commission was to make the word of God fully known and reveal the mystery that was hidden throughout the ages. This mystery, Paul wrote, is "Christ in you, the hope of glory" (Colossians 1:27 NRSV). When you realize that Christ is dwelling in you, life is never the same.

Back in Emmaus, after Jesus disappeared, the disciples said to each other, "Didn't our hearts feel strangely warm as he talked with us on the road and explained the Scriptures to us?" (Luke 24:32).This is what happens when you truly see the meaning of Scripture, it settles in your heart, and you know that Christ dwells in your heart through faith (see Ephesians 3:17 NRSV).

. . .

Sensitize me, I ask you Lord,

so I can know you

in the breaking of the bread.

> *Enoch walked with God;*
> *then he was no more,*
>
> *because God took him.*
> Genesis 5:24 NRSV

O Jesus, I Have Promised

Words: John Ernest Bode

Music: James William Elliott

O Je - sus, I have prom - ised To serve Thee to the end:

Be Thou for - ev - er near me, My Mas - ter and my friend;

I shall not fear the bat – tle, If Thou art by my side,

Nor wan - der from the path – way, If Thou wilt be my guide.

O JESUS, I HAVE PROMISED

O Jesus, I have promised to serve Thee to the end;
Be Thou forever near me, my Master and my Friend;
I shall not fear the battle if Thou art by my side,
Nor wander from the pathway if Thou wilt be my Guide.

O let me feel Thee near me! The world is ever near;
I see the sights that dazzle, the tempting sounds I hear;
My foes are ever near me, around me and within;
But Jesus, draw Thou nearer, and shield my soul from sin.

O let me hear Thee speaking in accents clear and still,
Above the storms of passion, the murmurs of self will.
O speak to reassure me, to hasten or control;
O speak, and make me listen, Thou Guardian of my soul.

I will show you
a still more
excellent way.
1 Corinthians 12:31 NRSV

MANY times I've sung this song in tears. I really have promised to serve Christ to the end. And over the years I have reviewed—in my thoughts, my prayers, in the Scriptures—what the phrase "serve the Lord" truly means. So I am glad to come back to this hymn and think about it again.

Two stories rise from the gospels which, in my opinion, best illustrate service to God. Both feature Mary of Bethany. The first tells that when Jesus was in Bethany he stayed at the home of Simon, who had leprosy. The disease made Simon an utter outcast from society. His handicap meant that he could do nothing for Jesus in terms of service. Then, during supper, a woman came in with a beautiful jar of expensive perfumed oil. She anointed Christ's head with the oil. The woman was Mary.

Some of the disciples were indignant. "What a waste of money," they said. "She could have sold that perfume for a fortune and given the money to the poor." Their idea of service could be measured in dollars, clearly seen and understood. But Jesus told them, "You will always have the poor among you [in fact, they were at that moment sitting in the house of the poor], and you can help them whenever you want to. But I will not be here with you much longer." Jesus asked the disciples, in effect, "Why do you trouble this woman? She has performed a good service for me." Mary served the Lord by loving him and she wasn't about to miss the opportunity to show her love (see Mark 14:3–9). If you will sing "O Jesus I Have Promised" you may see that, although it mentions service, the poet's impulse is her love for Jesus.

Here is the second gospel story about service to God. It is found in Luke's gospel. Jesus and the disciples were on their way to Jerusalem when they came to the village of Bethany where a woman named Martha welcomed them into her home. Her sister's name was Mary—the same woman who had anointed the Lord with the expensive perfumed oil. She sat at the Lord's feet, listening to what he said. But Martha was worrying over the meal she was preparing for her guests. She came to Jesus and said, "Lord, doesn't it seem unfair to you that my sister just sits here while I do all the work? Tell her to come and help me."

But the Lord said to her, "My dear Martha, you are so upset over all these details! There is only one thing worth being concerned about. Mary has discovered it—and I won't take it away from her"(see Luke 10:38–42).

What had Mary discovered? Love the Lord, and don't wait.

Do you think this means we should do nothing? No, it doesn't. Jesus didn't say the disciples should neglect the poor. But If I could give everything I have to the poor and even sacrifice my body for them, God expects that the impulse for this service be my love for Jesus Christ. Without such love my so-called service is of no value whatsoever in God's purpose (see 1 Corinthians 13:3).

I love you Lord because you loved me first
and gave your Son as a sacrifice for my sins.
I love you Lord, but all the love is yours,
and I live by your love.

"*Teacher,*
which is the most
important commandment
in the law of Moses?"

Jesus replied,

" '*You must love*
the Lord your God

with all your heart, all your soul,
and all your mind.' This is the first and greatest
commandment. A second is equally important:

'*Love your neighbor as yourself.*'"
Matthew 22:36–39

I Need Thee Every Hour

Words: Annie S. Hawks
Refrain: Robert Lowry

Music: Robert Lowry

I need Thee ev-'ry hour, Most gra-cious Lord;

No ten-der voice like Thine Can peace af-ford.

Refrain

I need Thee, O I need Thee; Ev-'ry hour I need Thee!

O bless me now, my Sav-ior, I come to Thee.

I NEED THEE EVERY HOUR

I need Thee every hour, most gracious Lord;
No tender voice like Thine can peace afford.

I need Thee every hour, stay Thou nearby;
Temptations lose their power when Thou art nigh.

I need Thee every hour, in joy or pain;
Come quickly and abide, or life is in vain.

I need Thee every hour; teach me Thy will;
And Thy rich promises in me fulfill.

Refrain
I need Thee, O I need Thee;
Every hour I need Thee;
O bless me now, my Savior,
I come to Thee.

As the deer pants for streams
of water,

so I long for you, O God.

I thirst for God, the living God.
When can I come and stand before him?

Day and night, *I have only tears for food,*
while my enemies continually taunt me, saying,
"Where is this God of yours?"

Psalm 42:1–3

ANNIE Sherwood Hawks wrote the lyrics for "I Need Thee Every Hour." Her poems first began being published when she was fourteen years old. She eventually wrote four hundred hymns; most of them were for use in Sunday schools. She married in 1857, lived in Brooklyn, New York, and attended the Hanson Place Baptist Church. There, Robert Lowry, who wrote the Score for "I Need Thee Every Hour," was the pastor.

This hymn expresses the heart of a real seeker of God. There is such a seeker in the poetry of the Song of Solomon, an astounding scriptural account of love between a young man and woman. "I sought him whom my soul loves," says the young woman. "I sought him but found him not; I called him, but he gave no answer" (3:1 NRSV). This is a common experience of believers, seekers, and lovers of Christ. Simply put, it is the experience of "Where did he go?" Annie Hawks probably experienced it. Have you?

There was a sixteenth-century Spanish Roman Catholic reformer, mystic, and poet named John of the Cross. He wrote a classic of world literature–*Dark Night of the Soul.* John knew the experience of seeking yet not finding the Lord. The following is a paraphrase of a portion of his book about the Song of Solomon, *Commentary of the Spiritual Canticle:*

I sought him but I did not find him (see Song of Solomon 3:1). You ask: Since the one I love is within me, why don't I find him or experience him?

Here is the reason: He remains concealed because you do not also hide yourself in order to meet and experience him. Anyone who wants to find a hidden treasure must enter the hiding place secretly. Then she will be hidden just as the treasure is hidden. To find him, forget all your possessions and all creation and hide in the interior, secret chamber of your spirit. There, closing the door behind you, pray to your Father in secret (see Matthew 6:6). Hidden with him you will experience him in hiding; love and enjoy him in hiding. You will delight with him in a way transcending all language and feeling.

The secret place John of the Cross is talking about is very hard to describe. The Bible resorts to poetic images in the Song of Solomon, the Psalms, and elsewhere to describe the place where our relationship with God is realized.

Here is what Jesus said about it: "I am the true vine, and my Father is the gardener. Remain in me, and I will remain in you. For a branch cannot produce fruit if it is severed from the vine, and you cannot be fruitful apart from me. Yes, I am the vine; you are the branches. Those who remain in me, and I in them, will produce much fruit. For apart from me you can do nothing" (John 15:1, 4–5).

The hiding place where a believer can love and enjoy God is like the very spot where a branch is connected to a vine. There the flow of the life of the vine enters the branch. This is why Jesus advised, "When you pray, go away by yourself, shut the door behind you, and pray to your Father secretly. Then your Father, who knows all secrets, will reward you" (Matthew 6:6).

. . .

O God, give me grace to forget all

my possessions and all the rest of creation.

Show me where and how to hide in the

interior, secret chamber of my spirit where

the flow of the vine enters the branch.

Let me experience you in this way.

Bend down, O Lord,
and hear my prayer;

answer me,
for I need your help.

Protect me, for I am devoted to you.
Save me, for I serve you and trust you.
You are my God.

Be merciful, O Lord,

for I am calling on you constantly.
Give me happiness, O Lord,
for my life depends on you.
Psalm 86:1–4

Nearer, My God, to Thee

Words: Sarah F. Adams

Music: Anonymous

Near - er, my God, to Thee, Near - er to Thee!

E'en though it be a cross That rais - eth me;

Still all my song shall be, Near - er, my God, to Thee,

Near - er, my God, to Thee, Near - er to Thee.

NEARER, MY GOD, TO THEE

Nearer, my God, to Thee, nearer to Thee!
E'en though it be a cross that raiseth me,
Still all my song shall be, nearer, my God, to Thee.

Though like the wanderer, the sun gone down,
Darkness be over me, my rest a stone.
Yet in my dreams I'd be nearer, my God to Thee.

There let the way appear, steps unto heav'n;
All that Thou sendest me, in mercy given;
Angels to beckon me nearer, my God, to Thee.

Refrain
Nearer, my God, to Thee,
Nearer to Thee!

> *"His purpose in all of this*
> *was that the nations*
> *should seek after God*
> *and perhaps feel their way toward him and find him—*
>
> *though he is not far from any one of us."*
> Acts 17:27

THE STORIES told of Abraham, Isaac, Jacob, and his twelve sons are often used as allegories. Believers in God, reading their stories in later days, have used them to help interpret their own experiences. And still do. "Nearer My God to Thee" uses a story about Jacob to disclose a fierce determination to live closer to God.

You'll have to read for yourself how Jacob, the younger brother, stole the inheritance of his older brother Esau; how he feared for his life and fled the family home for a faraway place called

Paddan-aram where his uncle Laban lived. The story is told in Genesis 27.

Our story picks up in chapter 28. Imagine how sorrowful his banishment would have made Jacob. Not only did he leave his family, his was the only household in the land that worshiped God. It is likely that Jacob thought that in leaving his home place he was also leaving God. Because in those days gods had only local authority. The god of Gaza was not the god of Ashkelon; the god of Beersheba would not be the god of Bethel. The "deities" were gods of this or that hill, or town, or region. Jacob may not have understood that his father Isaac's God was unlike the gods of the people who lived in the surrounding country.

So "Jacob left Beersheba and traveled toward Haran. At sundown he arrived at a good place to set up camp and stopped there for the night" (Genesis 28:10–11). Would Jacob's prayers be heard in this strange place? It is clear that Jacob was in a hard place—why else would he use a stone for a pillow as he lay down to sleep? "As he slept, he dreamed of a stairway that reached from earth to heaven. And he saw the angels of God going up and down on it. At the top of the stairway stood the LORD, and he said, 'I am the LORD, the God of your grandfather Abraham and the God of your father, Isaac" (vv. 12–13).

God repeated promises previously given to Jacob's father and grandfather and then added, "I will be with you, and I will protect you wherever you go. I will someday bring you safely back to this land. I will be with you constantly until I have finished giving you everything I have promised."

Then Jacob woke up and said, "Surely the LORD is in this place, and I wasn't even aware of it" (vv. 15–16). There are many messages in Genesis 28–the meaning of Jacob's dream, of God's promises, Bethel, the house of God, and Jacob's vow. But for today, let us revel in the realization that God is with us in all places.

I confess that, like Jacob, I sometimes find myself sleeping through the difficulties of my life. Because it seems to me that I am sleeping on a stone, I feel far from God's love. But this is not true. My stone pillow causes me to forget of the truth that God is everywhere and involved in all things. I pray that at these times I will wake like Jacob and exclaim, "Surely the Lord is in this place, and I wasn't even aware of it. . . . What an awesome place this is! It is none other than the house of God–the gateway to heaven!" (vv. 16–17).

Lord, I take your promise to be with me and keep me in the way that I should go—that you will give me bread to eat and clothing to wear so that I will, in the end, come to your house in peace and you shall be my God.

"But everything exposed by the light
becomes visible,
*for everything that becomes
visible is light.*

This is why it is said,
    'Awake,
        O sleeper,

    rise up from the dead,
and Christ will give you light.' "
Ephesians 5:13–14 NRSV, NLT

HYMNS OF DEVOTION
CD TRACK LISTING

1 Take My Life and Let it Be–Flute & Guitar (2:30)

2 Fill Thou My Life–Harp & Strings (3:31)

3 Jesus, I Come–Cello (3:20)

4 Just As I Am–Classical Piano (3:17)

5 I Am Thine, O Lord–Saxophone (2:06)

6 May the Mind of Christ My Savior–Cello (2:22)

7 Who Is on the Lord's Side?–Harp & Strings (4:16)

8 I Am Trusting Thee, Lord Jesus–Flute & Guitar (2:43)

9 O Master, Let Me Walk with Thee–Cello (2:11)

10 O Jesus, I Have Promised–Classical Piano (2:55)

11 I Need Thee Every Hour–Saxophone (3:12)

12 Nearer, My God, to Thee–Celtic Sounds (3:02)